ROSEMARY RADFORD RUETHER

THREE MEDIEVAL MYSTICS

VISIONARY WOMEN

FORTRESS PRESS
MINNEAPOLIS

Contents

VISIONARY WOMEN

Preface

It is with great pleasure that I introduce this publication, which makes my writings on three medieval mystics—Hildegard of Bingen, Mechthild of Magdeburg, and Julian of Norwich—accessible to a popular audience. The writings of these women were largely unknown until a few decades ago. Translations of medieval writers into English or other modern languages focused on the male theologians and generally did not see women as having an authoritative voice. We owe it to the new interest in women and women's writings in recent years that these women mystics have been rediscovered and their work made accessible in modern translations.

The rich creativity of the thought of these medieval women is providing Christians in the twenty-first century with new insights into Christian faith and into the medieval world as well. We are amazed at the range and complexity of female imagery in their work. Female images inform their understanding of God, the creation and redemption of the universe, the fecundity of nature, and the relation of the self to God. Such a range of female symbolism belongs more to the mystical than the scholastic tradition and was particularly developed by women mystics. Without these writings our understanding of the possibilities of feminine symbolism in Christianity would remain unknown to most Christians.

How did such women manage to write at all, much less have their writings preserved so that we can delight in their insights today? Officially medieval Christianity saw women as secondary in nature and sinful through their primacy in the Fall, therefore to be denied any public voice as teachers in the church. Yet the church also preserved the tradition that women were equally capable of holiness and might be empowered by the Holy Spirit as prophets to teach the church. This view of the Holy Spirit as an "equal opportunity employer" allowed medieval women to rupture the limits placed upon them and proclaim their visions boldly.

Yet their voices would still not have come down to us if there had not been a network of supporters around them that mentored these women, provided them with access to literacy and scholarship, encouraged them to write down their thoughts or acted as their secretaries to inscribe their visions, recognized them as prophetic thinkers, and advocated for their recognition as such to church authorities. Our knowledge of these women also depends on the religious communities of women and men who copied their works, preserved them in their libraries, and handed them down to future generations.

A great network of supporters, preservers, and publicists of the work of these three and other medieval women mystics surround them and allow us to enjoy them today. One thinks of Jutta, Hildegard's mentor, who educated her and promoted her to be her successor as abbess; of Volmar, the provost of the adjoining men's monastery, who recognized her gifts and acted as her scribe to write them down; and of her community of nuns, who translated her visions into brilliant pictures and preserved them in their community. One thinks of Heinrich of Halle, who likewise encouraged Mechthild and helped her write her visions; and of the nuns of the monastery of Helfta, who protected her in her old age and preserved her writings. One thinks of the Augustinian friars across the road from Julian's anchorhold, who lent her books for her study; and of the Benedictine monks who fled with her writings at the Reformation to keep them from being destroyed.

It is through such networks of lovers, preservers, and publicists of these women's work that the fruits of their spirit reach us today. Fortress Press now joins this network that keeps their memory alive. May they become ever more a part of our active tradition!

Introduction

The New Testament and patristic message of the inclusion of women in the image of God redeemed in Christ, however andro-centrically conceived and in dichotomous tension with women's subjugation in creation and fallenness, activated women as agents in seeking and acting on this offer or redemption. One discerns this presence of the female subject behind many New Testament and patristic male authors, either when men seek to contain and limit this female agency or when they appeal to women's particular interests; that is, promotion of asceticism to women as freeing them from the trials of male domination and childbearing.[1] But one seldom hears the voices of these women directly.

A few scraps remain of women's own words: some oracular cries from the Montanist prophets; something from the prison diary of the martyr

Perpetua; the Christian story cast into the schoolbook form of lines from Virgil by the fourth-century Roman matron Proba; a holy land travelogue by the late-fourth-century nun Egeria; some letters, poems and a martyr's life by the fifth-century empress Eudocia; and a few other letters, poems, epitaphs, and inscriptions.[2] But mostly we must try to discern the contours of female lives and thought through the eyes of their male friends. We can assume that Macrina thought about the Christian life much as her brother Gregory describes, but we can never know how key points might be nuanced by her woman's perspective.

Of the great ascetic foundresses of the fourth and fifth centuries, Macrina, Marcella, the Paulas and Melanias Elder and Younger, we have scarcely a line, even though we know from their male friends that they pursued studies of Scripture and of the church fathers and wrote extensively in the form of letters of inquiry on exegetical points, as well as interventions in doctrinal and church disputes.[3] The reasons for this lack of preservation of writings of the church mothers are not hard to find. The lack reflects the limits imposed upon their authority by their brothers, the church fathers.

Women may be equal in holiness and ultimately in heaven. A woman may even be learned, so much so that priests seek out her counseling on points of

Scripture, theology, and the spiritual life, as Gregory of Nyssa bowed to his sister as his mentor. But women may not teach publicly. Women's words of counsel and inspiration are to remain private. They are excluded from the public teaching of the church. Ergo, however much their memory and even their relics are venerated as saints, their writings are not preserved as official tradition.[4]

This situation of women's lack of public teaching authority in the church continued in the Middle Ages and was renewed in the Reformation. Indeed it has only begun to be overcome in the late twentieth century. But for various reasons its implications for the lack of preservation of women's writings began to change. Starting in the tenth century with the plays of Hrotsvit of Gandersheim, growing in the eleventh century and becoming a mighty stream in the twelfth to fifteenth centuries, we find more and more women's writings. These women write in a variety of genres, not just letters and saint's lives, but plays, theological treatises, guides to the spiritual life and, above all, accounts of their mystical experiences, the latter becoming women's particular genre of theological writing.

More and more women began to commit their thoughts to paper, often with the aid of a male scribe, and these writings were preserved. The reasons reflect the institutions of female religious life. There women learned elements of literacy in Latin and the vernacular. There they had libraries and scriptoria (which included painting and illumination) where their thoughts could be not only written down but preserved, copied, and sent to other readers. There through continual liturgical prayer, women might gain an extensive knowledge of Scripture and some theology, and could also express themselves in poems and plays to be put to music and performed liturgically in their communities—again to be written down, copied, circulated to other communities.

There remained from the New Testament legacy an important exception to women's lack of public teaching authority in Christianity, an exception that women used to gain a public voice in the medieval church. Although women could not be priests, they could be prophets.[5] God might speak directly to a woman, conveying an urgent message to the church and society of her time. Women might experience God in revelatory disclosures that could direct others on the path of holiness. In these roles as direct vehicles of God's presence and voice, women both denounced evils and pointed to the way of restored life with God.

Women's revelatory experiences were not self-validating. They had to be validated by male ecclesiastical authority—a personal counselor, an abbot, a bishop, even the Pope, the higher the rank the better. Visionary women who failed to gain such male support (or male support of sufficiently high rank and influence) could hardly gain a voice. When male authorities were divided on women's prophetic authenticity, which authorities won determined whether a woman and her writings were circulated and preserved or suppressed or even burned at the stake along with her body. When a woman claimed revelations, the critical question was from whence came these communications, God or the devil? Was she therefore a prophet or a witch? And, as in the case of Joan of Arc, which men had the power to make the crucial decision?[6]

Hildegard of Bingen

In the twelfth century, Hildegard was the most notable example of a woman who received such validation from the highest authorities of church and state. Thus she was able to exercise her extraordinary creative powers to the fullest extent, within the limits of the roles available to her of abbess and prophet. Hildegard's long life of eighty-one years covered most of the twelfth century, 1098–1179. Born as the tenth child to a noble family, well connected to political and church leaders, in Bermersheim bei Alzey in Rhine-Hessen, she was given to the church as a tithe at the age of eight, being entrusted to the care of Jutta of Sponheim, a noblewoman, whose hermitage was attached to the male Benedictine monastery of Saint Disibod. There Hildegard gained a thorough grounding in the Latin Bible, particularly through the monastic office.

Although she claims that both her mentor, Jutta, and she herself remained "unlearned," it is evident from her subtle and masterful but idiosyncratic Latin that she was able to explore a range of authorities on theology and natural history of her time. But she remained largely self-taught both in developing her distinctive exposition of the orthodox Christian worldview and in her use of imagery, music, and language. Hildegard regarded her language as itself revelatory and issued stern warnings against any editor who might revise it, beyond grammatical corrections. She also developed a secret language, based on Latin, which was used as a mystical form of communication in her community.[1]

In her *Life*, written at her dictation when she was in her mid-seventies, Hildegard recounts that from earliest childhood she had luminous visionary experiences, a second sight into hidden realities that took place while she retained ordinary consciousness. These visions were vividly pictorial, although also interpreted to her in Latin, in such a form that both the vision and its meaning were clearly imprinted on her memory.[2] These visions were accompanied by debilitating illnesses "that threatened to bring me to death's door."[3] When she realized as a small child that others did not see as she saw, she learned to keep silent about such experiences, communicating them privately to her mentor, Jutta. In her fortieth year the pain of suppressing these visions became so great that she divulged them to Volmar, the monastery provost, who encouraged her to write them down.[4]

The hermitage with Jutta and Hildegard attracted many other women members and grew into a well-endowed cloister, attached to the male community of Saint Disibod. When Jutta died in 1136 Hildegard was elected its head. It was in 1141, when Hildegard was forty-two years old, that she received visions of fiery light that gave her an infused knowledge of the Scriptures, Old and New Testaments, accompanied by a heavenly voice commanding her to "say and write what you see and hear."[5] With the editorial assistance of Volmar and her favorite nun of her community, Richardis von Stade, Hildegard began to dictate these visions, together with the exegesis of their meaning that came to her through the heavenly voice.

Over the next ten years, 1141–51, her first major book, *Scivias*, took shape. Eventually each vision in its visual form would be painted, probably at Hildegard's dictation, by women who did the illuminations in the monastery scriptoria.[6] Thus we have each of the twenty-six visions in the *Scivias* in three forms: described in words, in a painting in vivid colors, and interpreted by the heavenly voice. These twenty-six visions, divided into three books, comprise a comprehensive theological cosmology, a *summa theologica* that touches on the entire range of topics of salvation history from beginning to end.[7]

In the *Scivias* we are led through complex pictorial images, which are then exegeted: God's creation of the world; Lucifer's fall; Adam and Eve's fall from paradise; the incarnation of the Word who created the world taking human flesh in the womb of the Virgin Mary to heal the breach opened up between God and humans; the course of salvation history from Adam's fall, Noah, Abraham, and Moses, the patriarchs and prophets, then the apostles and martyrs of early Christianity; to the building of the church in her own day, with the struggles between faithful and unfaithful Christians, to the anticipation of the final conflicts with the Antichrist, the judgment and transformation of creation into its eschatological form, culminating in heaven and hell beyond the present temporal order.

Although Hildegard receives and exegetes this story seriatim in visions and discourses that begin with creation, go on through salvation history and end with eschatology, there is a sense both in the *Scivias* and in its redoing in her final great work (written in her late seventies), *The Book of Divine Works*, that this salvational drama is present in her mind as a unified whole, all simultaneously here and now, from the perspective of God who stands outside time, a simultaneity that Hildegard partially shares as one caught up in vision to the divine viewpoint. Again and again in her letters she will sketch this whole drama in a few powerful strokes: Lucifer's fall, the paradisial and then fallen condition of Adam, Christ taking on human flesh in the virgin's womb, the final conflict between God and Satan, all brought to bear on the present condition of the church as both the community of redemption and devil-ridden in its human weakness and strife.[8]

Modern interpreters of Hildegard have been particularly struck by her habitual method of affirming her prophetic authority as a vehicle of God, while simultaneously discounting herself as a "poor little female figure" (*paupercula feminea forma*),[9] physically weak, unlearned, without status as fallen Eve. From a modern and feminist perspective that sees self-affirmation as crucial to women's well-being, this constant dichotomy between Hildegard's diminishment as a woman and God's authority seems either internalized self-hatred or a rhetorical trick or perhaps some of both. But this puzzle reflects modern anthropological views that disappear once the assumptions of Hildegard and her context are taken seriously.

We should recognize at least four levels of meaning that dictate this dichotomy between Hildegard as "poor little female figure" and the divine that speaks through her as prophet. First, as indicated above, this was the only way a woman could gain a public voice in medieval Christianity. As one under subjugation in creation and domination in the fall, a woman could not publicly teach theologically or exercise authority in her own name, but only as one whose subjugation had been overridden by a God who used her as a vehicle of revelation to raise her beyond both her female condition and the human condition in general. As prophet a woman has authority not in her own name, but as one used by God despite her "weakness." Thus in utilizing this contrast between her feminine weakness and the revelatory voice of God that speaks through her, Hildegard simply accepts and conforms to the view of her church, which negates her as a woman only to allow her to speak with the highest and most thunderous authority possible as voice of God.

Once validated as a true prophet, however, Hildegard could and did speak with precisely such a thunderous voice to the greatest men of her day. And this voice of divine authority was generally accepted by these men, despite the conflicts some had with her. Many sought her out humbly, asking for her prayers, her insights about the future, whether God had told her anything about them, about the fate of souls in the next life, and about cures for the infertile and the demon-possessed. Once the authenticity of her divine voice was accepted, her female "weakness" was not so much an impediment as a marvel, a continual affirmation of the scriptural principles that "the Spirit blows where it will" (John 3:8) and "God chose what is weak in the world to shame the strong" (1 Cor. 1:27).[10]

Second, for Hildegard this self-negation corresponds to the human condition generally. All humans are "ashes of ashes, filth of filth,"[11] both in the created body apart from God's vivifying power and as fallen into captivity to this identity as "ashes and slime" in sin. Humans, male or female, cannot expect to speak truth or live in a holy manner unless they empty themselves and allow God to use them as a vehicle of grace. In her letter to the younger woman mystic Elisabeth of Schönau, Hildegard makes clear that not only women, but all true Christian visionaries who hope to impart God's word to their fellow humans, can do so only if they empty themselves of any self-will. Not only she but the greatest prophets and apostles of Scripture, such as Paul, could be true vessels of God's word only to the extent that they acknowledged and made themselves "nothing," so God could be all in all in and through them.

Hildegard shows that this is the original and essential way all creation remains united with God, while the crux of fallenness is the assertion of self against God's life-giving presence:

> I am but a poor creature and a fragile vessel; yet what I speak to you comes not from me but from the clear light. Human beings are vessels God has made and filled with the Spirit so that the divine work might come to perfection in them. . . . It was through the divine word alone that everything came into existence perfect. The grasses, the woods, the trees came forth. The sun too and the moon and the stars went to their appointed places to perform their service. . . . It was only humans themselves who did not know their creator. For although God bestowed great knowledge on humans, they raised themselves up in their hearts and turned away from God. . . . But God endowed some persons with insight so that humankind should not completely fall into derision.[12]

Hildegard alludes to Abel, to the Hebrew seers, and finally to the coming of Christ as the mending of this relation to God. But in her own day there had been a steady decline of the human grasp of this life-giving presence. It was, as Hildegard calls it, a "womanish time" (a time of lack of virtue), and so God was lifting up new prophets, even women, to be divine instruments. To be true instruments, persons such as herself and Elizabeth had to avoid the devilish temptations to claim such authority as their own, rather than making themselves humble vehicles of God:

> Those who long to bring God's words to completion must always remember that, because they are human, they are vessels of clay and so should continually focus on what they are and what they will be. . . . They themselves only announce the mysteries like a trumpet that which indeed allows the sound but is not itself the source that produces the note.[13]

On a third level, Hildegard accepts this dichotomy between her weakness and the divine authority that speaks in her because it corresponds to her personal experience of herself. Hildegard knows herself to be physically assailed by continual illness, of inadequate learning, marginal as a woman in her church and society, and yet empowered by extraordinary energy that even in old age can make her feel like a young girl.[14] She has visionary knowledge that can see the whole cosmos and world history from end to end in a glance; she is endowed with gifts in music, language, sciences, and with enormous willpower to contend with the greatest powers of church and state in her day. While we might say both voices and energies are Hildegard's, she herself could explain the duality in her experience, and assure that the second voice was accepted by her society, only by assuming that the first was herself, while the second was God acting in her.

On a fourth level, subordinate to the first three, Hildegard wields the contrast between her littleness and the divine voice rhetorically, as a power tool by which she not only sets forth her visions but also contends with adversaries in her church and society and responds to humble requests from petitioners who seek her prayers and advice. Nor is she above using this duality ironically, as a putdown to the great men of her day who assume that their maleness, combined with high class and ecclesiastical status, automatically makes them the voice of God.

Hildegard's last great struggle at the end of her life was against the prelates of Mainz, who imposed an interdict on her community because she refused to exhume the body of a man buried in her monastic cemetery who they claimed (and she denied) had died excommunicate. Hildegard threatened the prelates with divine judgment, contrasting their own exemplification of "womanish times" with her divinely given authority as God's *bellatrix* (female warrior):

And I heard a voice saying thus: Who created Heaven? God. Who opens heaven to the faithful? God. Who is like Him? No one. And so, O men of faith, let none of you resist Him or oppose Him, lest He fall on you in His might and you have no helper to protect you from His judgment. This time is a womanish time, because the dispensation of God's justice is weak. But the strength of God's justice is exerting itself, a female warrior battling against injustice, so that it might fall defeated.[15]

All Hildegard's writings from her forties to her seventies, following her vision of the voice that commanded her to "say and write what you see and hear," show absolute confidence in this voice as God speaking through her. Her success in having this voice authenticated by the highest ecclesiastical authorities provided an essential condition for her ability to wield it in her society. After confiding her visions privately to Jutta and Volmar, she wrote to the greatest monk of her day, Bernard of Clairvaux, in 1146, several years into the writing of her *Scivias*, to seek his approbation of her visionary authority. Bernard's reply to this appeal, from one who was at that time an unknown nun, was perfunctory but affirmative, urging her to "recognize this gift as a grace" and to respond to it eagerly but also humbly.[16]

In 1146–47, by a lucky stroke of fortune, Pope Eugenius III, a Cistercian and disciple of Bernard, was meeting in synod in Trier. Volmar had told his abbot, Kuno, of Hildegard's visions; Kuno informed Heinrich, archbishop of Mainz. Heinrich mentioned this to the pope, who dispatched two legates for a copy of the incomplete *Scivias*. Bernard intervened to affirm Hildegard's authenticity to Pope Eugenius, who was impressed and read parts of the text before the assembled prelates. He then wrote a letter to Hildegard giving her his apostolic approbation.[17]

So, by a fortuitous chain of male ecclesiastical approval, Hildegard was able to gain the highest validation in the church. She also gained protection over her monastery by then-emperor Frederick Barbarossa. Despite her later denunciations of him, this protection held firm throughout her life.[18] Hildegard's divine voice was thus credentialed by the highest authorities of her time. She would maintain this authority, despite private doubts by some, through several crucial battles with church authorities, in which she did not spare her denunciations of the corruption she saw in the lives of great prelates and princes.

In at least one of these conflicts, when Hildegard claimed divine mandate to move her community to a new site at Rupertsberg, freeing it from dependence on Saint Disibod, she reports that some questioned her authority and even her sanity:

Many people said, "What's all this—so many hidden truths revealed to this foolish, unlearned woman, when there are many brave and wise men around? Surely this will come to nothing!" For many people wondered whether my revelation stemmed from God, or from the parchedness of aerial spirits that often seduced human beings.[19]

Hildegard's theological anthropology of gender in creation, fall, and redemption is not easy to sort out with precision, for she was an imagistic thinker, not a philosophical systematician. But the general pattern of her thought can be summarized. First, she herself and all women, in relation to God as God's creation, are simply and complexly *homo*, fully and completely equivalent to men as expressions of the image and likeness of God. Characteristically, when God speaks to her, as when she speaks to others (mostly men) in the voice of God, she is referred to simply as "O man" (*O homo*). God does not address her as a woman, even in affectionate terms, such as daughter, handmaiden, or the like, but simply as a human person.[20]

For Hildegard the original Adamic nature was dual, being made from "wet mud" (*limosa terra*) and filled with God's vivifying spirit, which Hildegard calls *veriditas* or "greening power," a term she uses for the whole cosmos as filled with God's life-giving power.[21] As originally filled by the Spirit, Adam was glorious, endowed with divine knowledge and harmony that expressed itself in a beautiful singing voice (a distinctively Hildegardian touch).[22] Eve shared in this same nature, while as woman she was also created to be mother to their joint offspring.

In the original paradisial state Adam and Eve would have made love virginally. Lust would have been absent, but there would have been the sweetest pleasure, communicated in a nongenital embrace and "sweat" passed between their sleeping bodies. Eve would have given birth, not through her vagina but through her side, as she herself had been born from Adam's side, and thus would have remained virgin in impregnation and parturition. This original virginal impregnation and birth were restored in Christ's birth from Mary and are represented in the church born from the side of Christ.[23]

Adam lost the fullness of his vivifying power, however, by seeking to grasp his own self-will, rather than making himself simply an instrument of God's indwelling Spirit, although this life-giving Spirit remains the true life principle of humans. For Hildegard, the primary cause is not human, male or female, but the jealousy of the devil. Prior to the creation of humans, God created the angels. But part of the angelic hosts, led by Lucifer, tried to seize God's glory and fell from heaven, becoming the source of all diabolic plotting against divine life. Unlike humans, Lucifer fell utterly, losing all capacity for goodness and becoming wholly evil.[24]

God then created humans from clay and filled them with life. God planned that this new creation would replace the fallen angels. The devil, utterly antagonistic to Adam and his offspring (which Eve carried in her body like stars), plotted to deceive the couple. He hated Adam's sweet singing voice and the harmonious life of paradise, and so the devil sought to destroy it, to get humans into his power by deceiving them. The devil came to Eve because, in her innocence, she was more susceptible to being misled and also because Adam would accept her suggestion out of his love for her. But Hildegard sees these aspects in the primal misstep as modifying its gravity. Adam and Eve are more childish and victimized than evil. They do not fall wholly, as does Lucifer, and thus can be reclaimed by God. In a striking image, Hildegard pictures Adam as turning from God by *failing* to pluck the flower of obedience to God and so losing the indwelling spirit.[25]

Once fallen and ejected from paradise, Adam and Eve have lost their original harmoniousness, and their knowledge of God is dimmed. Their sexuality is corrupted into lust, although Hildegard sees this as more a male than a female characteristic. Women, she believes, are naturally averse to the sexual act and only experience some sexual lust after they have been introduced to it by men.[26] Most of all, the fallen world is one buffeted by the constant attacks of the devil, who seeks to get God's human creature wholly in his power. But God from the beginning sends vehicles of divine grace, starting with Abel and Noah.

Hildegard's view of human nature is more that of the "two tendencies" than an Augustinian loss of free will. The vices, agents of the devil, seek to pull humans one way, while the sweet voices of the virtues (typically presented as feminine)[27] recall humans to their true glory. God's project of restoration of humans culminates in the birth of Christ, who takes human flesh from the Virgin Mary and thus restores that original form of humanity in which human flesh is a perfectly receptive instrument of the divine Spirit. All Christians share this restored human nature through rebirth in the womb of mother church and through feeding on the sacrament of Christ's eucharistic body.

Hildegard's view of woman as woman, in relation to man as male, is double-sided. Physically and socially she accepts gender hierarchy as the created order, although she also hints that men use the claim that women are punished for Eve's sin to unjustly oppress them.[28] But women as women are assumed to be physically weaker than men and in need of their protection. Also, for Hildegard, the biological complementarity of the male as sower of the seed and women as nurturer of it dictates a hierarchical social order that demands that women as wives obey their husbands.[29]

This difference in male and female roles is continued in the church in the exclusion of women as priests. These "natural" male and female social roles, parallel to males as begetters and women as conceivers, should not be confused by cross-dressing or by women taking on male roles.[30] In a similar way Hildegard accepts class hierarchy in her society and sees this as a reflection of natural hierarchy, the hierarchy of the angels, as well as the difference between species of animals. She bristles in defense of her own practice of admitting only women of noble birth to her monastery, when this is challenged by another abbess.[31]

While male and female complementarity dictates female subordination socially, on the cosmic level Hildegard sees a complementarity of masculine and feminine that manifests God's design for cosmic harmony. This cosmic complementarity is represented for Hildegard on many levels. Maleness represents God and God's word, while femaleness represents earth and flesh, the matter through which God shapes all things. Here flesh, matter or earth (*terra*) is not evil, but rather, in its "virginal" form, is the bodily substance that God's Spirit fills with life, moisture, and "greenness." The beauty and delight of God's creation lie in the harmonious union of these two principles, God's life-giving power and matter or *terra*.[32]

Wisdom (*Sapientia*) or Love (*Caritas*) is the feminine expression both of God and of creation, mediating the union between the two. Hildegard's final great work in her seventies, *The Book of Divine Works*, is a reworking of the whole drama of creation, incarnation, and redemption to focus on the role of Wisdom/Love, who mediates between God and creation. It is through Wisdom/Love that God created the cosmos in the beginning, and it is in Wisdom/Love that God will bring it to completion in the end.[33] The axis of this union of God and flesh mediated by Wisdom is the incarnation of the Word through the Virgin Mary, who gives the divine Word his humanness through her virginal flesh as one who is totally an instrument of the divine Spirit.[34]

Finally Ecclesia, bride of Christ and mother of Christians, who receives the vivifying power of Christ's redemptive sacrifice on the cross as her bridal "dowry," manifests this reunion of divine Spirit and virginal matter.[35] Ecclesia is pictured in many of

Hildegard's visions as a towering woman, holding reborn Christians in her arms and womb, while her head is assailed by corrupt and unfaithful church leaders.[36] In one vivid picture of the final conflict between God and the Antichrist, Ecclesia is even imaged as having the lower part of her body taken over by an ass's head protruding from her vagina.[37] But Christ will intervene to throw this final eruption of Satan into hell, while rescuing for paradise the faithful children reborn in the womb of mother church.

For Hildegard, Christian virgins are particular expressions of the true children of mother church. They are the reborn virgin Eve manifest in the Virgin Mary. In their holy life in community, Eden is partly restored. Hildegard even dressed her nuns in solemn liturgy in long white veils and golden crowns to symbolize their way of life as the restoration of Eden. She heard in the sweet music of liturgical chant an echo of the music of paradise.[38] In her letter to the prelates of Mainz imploring them to lift the interdict that had silenced liturgical music in her community, she suggests that these prelates imitate the devil, who ever seeks to silence music that reminds humans of paradise.[39]

Hildegard describes the music of paradise, lost in the fall but partly restored with the aid of musical instruments:

God, however, restores the souls of the elect to that pristine blessedness by infusing them with the light of truth. And in accordance with His eternal Plan, He so devised it that whenever He renews the hearts of many with the outpouring of the prophetic spirit, they might, by means of interior illumination, regain some of the knowledge which Adam had before he was punished for his sin. And so the holy prophets, inspired by the Spirit which they had received, were called . . . not only to compose psalms and canticles (by which the hearts of listeners were inflamed), but also to construct musical instruments to enhance these songs of praise with melodic strains. . . . In such a way these holy prophets get beyond the music of this exile and recall to mind that divine melody of praise which Adam, in company with the angels, enjoyed in God before the fall.[40]

Hildegard has no doubt that virginity or chastity is an essential expression of redeemed nature, the restored paradise and anticipated life in heaven when all death and suffering will be overcome. She strongly supports the Gregorian reforms that imposed celibacy on the priesthood. For her the various celibate ecclesiastical orders—priests, monks, and nuns—stand in a higher level of holiness than married laypeople, although ecclesiastics can also become instruments of the devil.[41]

Although she includes married laypeople in the redeemed, she sees them as a lower order who produce children for the church; she visualizes them as lying in the clouds in the lower part of Ecclesia's body, rather than in her bosom.[42] In her description of the final defeat of the devil and the gathering of the redeemed into the heavenly paradise, she speaks of prophets, apostles and martyrs, virgins and widows, anchorites and monks, and princes being gathered into heaven. Married lay commoners are too unimportant to mention.[43]

For Hildegard, gender difference is not annulled by Christ, but rather virginity annuls the fallen nature and restores the paradisial union of body and spirit of both men and women. Virginal women not only are included in equal honor in this procession of the redeemed, but they have special mysterious meaning as representatives of virginal Eve restored in Mary, the church as Virgin Mother of Christians, and finally that divine Wisdom and Love that ever unites God and matter in symphonic harmony in its once and future form, anticipated here and now in the virginal flesh and sweet song of vowed women religious.

Hildegard belongs to the early medieval world of rural monastic estates ruled by men and women of noble families; Aquinas to the university, mendicant orders, and emerging cities of the thirteenth century.

In the 1230s the major collection of canon law was promulgated, closing loopholes by which abbesses had exercised elements of pastoral office in the early Middle Ages. Women were strictly forbidden from public teaching or preaching, touching sacred vessels, incensing the altar, or taking communion to the sick. Spiritual guidance of nuns, including confession, and external control of finances of nunneries were more firmly put in the hands of supervising priests.[44]

While such matters were disputed in Hildegard's day, she was able to employ the combination of her prophetic office and her extensive connections with prelates and princes of noble families to wrest control of her own community from the monks of Saint Disibod, moving her monastery to another site, where she both governed its external affairs and controlled its pastoral and liturgical life. Although she still received a provost from Saint Disibod's, she prevailed in claiming that the nuns had the right to appoint this provost.[45]

Between 1158 and 1170 when she was in her sixties and seventies, she conducted four preaching tours throughout Germany, speaking to both clergy and laity in chapter houses and in public, mainly denouncing clerical corruption and calling for reform. We have the texts of several of such sermons, such as one she preached at Cologne in 1163.

Hildegard sent a copy of this sermon to Dean Philip and the cathedral chapter of Cologne, who humbly asked for it so they could reform their lives by careful study of her inspired words.[46]

By one hundred years later it was hard to imagine such acceptance of public preaching by a woman, even a well-connected abbess and acknowledged prophet. In the mid-fourteenth century Catherine of Siena would intervene with popes, prelates, and princes to end the Avignon captivity of the papacy and Great Schism, but she did so in a more private manner, by audiences and letters.[47] Women's religious writing would increase after the twelfth century, but the genre would be primarily personal spiritual experiences, not the sketching of a vast cosmology. The shift of scholarship from monasteries to universities (where women were barred from study) would also bring a decline in the educational level of nuns. Although the nuns of Helfta in the thirteenth century maintained university-level education for their women,[48] the Beguine mystic Mechthild of Magdeburg, who ended her days at Helfta, dictated her revelation in her Low German dialect, not Latin.

Mechthild of Magdeburg

With Mechthild of Magdeburg (1210–83), we enter a world of female visionary imagination and religious life different from Hildegard's, but also far removed from the intellectual world and university life of her contemporary Thomas Aquinas. Born in Saxony to a family of knightly class, Mechthild was well acquainted with the culture of princely courts, but also with the growing urban life and the new urban preaching and mendicant orders, the Dominicans and Franciscans, whom she saw as God's gift to reform a sinful age.[1]

Mechthild recounts her first "greeting" by the Holy Spirit when she was twelve; it was such an overwhelming experience that she could never thereafter tolerate giving in to any sin. These experiences continued daily.[2] When she was in her early twenties she joined a Beguine community in Magdeburg, where she lived for forty years. The Beguines represented a new form of female urban religious life in the thirteenth century in which groups of women took simple vows of chastity but were free to marry. They lived together in houses in the midst of urban life, supporting themselves through handwork and also serving their neighbors through charity, nursing the sick, and teaching. They fell under suspicion of heresy, mostly unfounded, through their uncloistered way of life but were valued by city fathers for their services; these officials often furnished some of the Beguines' support.[3]

Mechthild reflects this new context of women's religious life both in her compassion for the weak and suffering (in this life and in purgatory)[4] and in her sense of personal vulnerability to clerical foes who were offended by her claims of visionary authority.[5] Like Hildegard, Mechthild is certain of the truth of her visionary gifts and struggles against those who challenge it, but she lacks both the aristocratic hauteur and the access to the highest levels of power of church and state that protected the abbess.

When she was forty Mechthild received a command from God to write down her visions under the title of *The Flowing Light of the Godhead*.[6] Like Hildegard, Mechthild protests her unworthiness and lack of learning but affirms that God's demands take precedence over her weakness. She too consulted with her confessor, a Dominican, Heinrich of Halle, who both affirmed the divine origin of the command to write and copied down what she told him. Over the next twenty years Mechthild dictated a succession of revelations, which Heinrich organized into six books. The seventh book was dictated in her old age after she entered the convent of Helfta. Mechthild recorded her visions in her own Low German dialect. Heinrich of Halle, who organized the complete German version, also translated the whole into Latin about the time of her death.[7]

Although Mechthild was supported by her Dominican confessor and later by the aristocratic nuns of Helfta, she speaks often and bitterly of foes who challenged the veracity of her visions and her right to make them public through writing. When some men told her that her book should be burned, she took her complaint to God, who assured her that "the truth cannot be burned by anyone" and that her book was protected by God's own hand, which is stronger than any man's. In the vision God even identified her book with God's Trinitarian nature: the parchment on which it was written as God's humanity, the words that flew into her soul as God's divinity, and the voice of these words as the Holy Spirit.[8]

God's choice of such a lowly vessel to communicate God's revelations duplicates the kenosis or self-emptying of God in the incarnation, just as God chose to build "a golden house in this filthy slough, to live here with your mother and all creatures." Echoing Paul's principle that God chooses the lowly to confound the wise, Mechthild is told that many a wise master is a fool in God's eyes. Rather God typically imparts special graces to "the lowest, the least, the best concealed place," just as a mighty flood "flows by nature into the valley."[9]

Mechthild not only resists those who challenge her visions, but developed a general view of the state of Christianity of her day as corrupted by sinful clerics and religious. She perceives behind the façade of many "spiritual people" a hypocrisy and self-centeredness that not only fails to understand the true message of spiritual life, but corrupts others. Mechthild compares herself to Christ, who must drink the cup of gall created by these false Christians: "The Devil has many a cupbearer among spiritual people, cups so full of poison that they cannot drink it all alone but must pour out the bitterness for the children of God."[10] Such criticisms undoubtedly fueled some of the persecution that Mechthild experienced.

Mechthild shares with Hildegard and the orthodox Christianity of her day general assumptions about salvation history. Her theological world moves between the drama of God's creation of humanity and Adam and Eve's fall, through the faithful witnesses from Abel and the prophets to the central mystery of redemption through Mary and Christ, to the apostles and saints of mother church, to the present time when many church leaders "stain" the church through their corruption. For her too the coming drama of the Antichrist, the sufferings of the saints in that time, the final judgment and eternal transformation of the world loom just ahead.[11]

But where Hildegard's visions survey this historical and cosmic sweep, in Mechthild the focus is on the intense, intimate drama of the soul, Mechthild's own soul, in its ecstatic flight to and union with God as its beloved, and in its suffering alienation, which imitates the kenosis of Christ in tormented flesh, as the paradigmatic center of the salvation drama. In her description of this love drama between the soul and God, Mechthild draws on the heritage of Christian interpretation of the Song of Songs blended with elements drawn from the German *minnesinger* poetry of the love relation between a lady and her noble lord. The blending of these two traditions, the mystical reading of the Song of Songs and the poetry of courtly love, in Mechthild as well as other Beguine mystics, created a new genre of religious language, which Barbara Newman has called *mystique courtoise*.[12]

For Mechthild God's decision to create humanity is driven by desire to be fruitful and to love. In one vision Mechthild envisions the Trinity in conversation, deciding to create humanity as a Bride for God to love and be loved in return:

> Then the Eternal Son said with great politeness: "Dear Father, my nature, too, should bear fruit. . . . Let Us pattern mankind after Me, although I foresee great sorrow since I must love man eternally." The Father replied, "Son, I, too, am moved by a powerful desire in my breast, and I hear the sound of love. We shall become fruitful in order to be loved in return. . . . I will create Bride for Myself who shall greet Me with her mouth and wound Me with her look; only then will love begin." And the Holy Spirit said to the Father: "Yes, dear Father, I will bring the Bride to Your bed." . . . Then the Holy Trinity leaned over the creation of all things and created us, body and soul, with untold love.[13]

Adam and Eve together were given the noble nature of the Son. To Adam was given a share in the Son's wisdom and earthly power over all earthly creatures. To Eve was given the Son's "loving honorable modesty which He Himself bore in honor of his Father." "Their bodies were created pure, for God did not create anything to make them suffer shame, and they were dressed in angel's garments." Mechthild seems to share the Origenist view of the early Augustine that originally Adam and Eve would have conceived children in some ethereal and sinless manner that would not have changed the virginal nature of their bodies: "They were to conceive their children in holy love, as the sparkling sun shines on the water without troubling it."[14]

With sin, however, Adam and Eve lost this original sinless and incorruptible body. Their bodies became corruptible and sin-prone. In a dramatic image Mechthild speaks of the fallen body as having "sinful sap," "which Adam extracted from the apple, which flows naturally through all our limbs." Eve received in addition an accursed (menstrual) blood, "which began with Eve and all other women from the apple."[15]

Mechthild attributes to the fallen body both the tendency to sin—to turn from God and to indulge bodily desires—as well as finitude, pain, and illness. The soul in herself retains her natural likeness to God and thus her desire to ascend and reunite with God as her beloved. But her ties to the fallen body drag her down to the earthly realm and tempt her with desires for false loves of bodily indulgence. Yet in ecstatic experience the soul temporarily frees itself from its ties to the body and tastes its original and renewed love relation with God, which has been lost with the fall but restored through the incarnation of Christ in Mary's sinless flesh.

Mary, whose body was uncorrupted, preserved this original love relation of the soul with God during the period between the fall of Adam and the incarnation. Mary as God's bride exemplifies what God intended and continues to intend the soul to be. Thus Mary speaks:

> So the almighty Father chose me for a Bride, in order to have something to love, for His beloved Bride, the noble soul, was dead. . . . Then I alone became Bride of the Holy Trinity and the Mother of orphans, and brought them before the eyes of God, so they might not sink.

Mary is a mediatrix who mothers and suckles all the faithful with the "pure, unspoiled milk of true, tender mercy," not only Christ and Christians, but also the prophets and sages before Christ was born, and Mary continues to do so until the Day of Judgment.[16]

The soul can taste, at least in momentary glimpses, its true noble nature, and dance and play in heaven with its beloved. Again and again Mechthild describes this love play with its beloved in language drawn from courtly love as well as the Song of Songs. In one vision, the soul complains to *Minne*, or Lady Love, imagined as the go-between that captures and wounds her with desire. The dialogue ends with the soul acknowledging her defeat by Love, telling her to take a letter to her beloved: "Please tell my love that His bed is ready and I lovingly long for him."[17]

In another vision, the soul appears in court as a timid servant girl looking longingly at a prince. In imagery drawn from Sacred Heart and eucharistic devotions, God eagerly bares his red-hot heart to her and takes her into it. The two embrace and mingle together "like water and wine."[18] Although God is infinitely greater than the "poor soul," in the love relation they become equal. God even subjects himself to the soul and does her will, as the lord kneels to the lady in courtly love.[19] God's great love for the soul is a continual kenosis in which God pours himself out for the soul, so much so that God is as "lovesick" for her as she is for God: "She is consumed by Him and takes leave of herself; when she has had enough, he is more lovesick for her than He ever was before when He desired more."[20]

Although this love quest and play, culminating in mutual dissolution into one another, is the heart of Mechthild's visions, nevertheless, it can only be momentary as long as the soul is tied to the body. The soul must not only fall back into its distance from

God, but it must even embrace alienation from God as its highest self-abnegation of its own desires for the sake of love for God.[21] In this paradoxical move, Mechthild also sees the soul embracing innocent bodily suffering (although not sin) as the way to purify its attachment to the body and to participate in the crucifixion of Christ, who not only entered the flesh but suffered all the torments of the flesh to express his loving quest to redeem humanity's soul and body.[22]

Thus Mechthild describes her early ascetic efforts to subdue the body through fasting, flagellation, and vigils,[23] as well as sufferings that came to her through illness and, most of all, through betrayal and persecution by her foes, as imitation of Christ's redemptive suffering. Thus Christ speaks to Mechthild not only as bride, but as one who must share in his sufferings and so become his female counterpart as dying and rising Christ:

> You shall be martyred with Me, betrayed by envy, sought out by falsehood, captured by hatred, bound by slander, blindfolded so the truth may be withheld from you, slapped by the wrath of the world, brought before the court in confession, boxed on the ears with punishment, sent before Herod in court, undressed in wretchedness, flogged with poverty, crowned by temptation, looked down upon in degradation; you shall bear your cross despising sin, shall be crucified

renouncing all your desire, but nailed to the cross
with holy virtues; wounded by love, you shall die
on the cross with holy constancy, be pierced in your
heart by constant union, removed from the cross in
true victory over all your foes, buried in obscurity,
and finally, in a holy conclusion, you shall rise from
the death and ascend into heaven, drawn by God's
breath.[24]

In the salvation drama of humanity's creation,
fall, and redemption, Mechthild does not believe
that women are in any way inferior to men in their
spiritual nature. She suggests in her account of the
creation of Adam and Eve that the Son apportions his
gifts to the couple with wisdom and power for Adam
and love for Eve. Eve receives a double punishment
in the fall of cursed sap and cursed blood. Mechthild
accepts women's marginalized and powerless place
in society as a given but relates it, not to divine punishment, but rather to divine favor, giving women
greater likelihood of sharing Christ's sufferings and
receiving God's grace, which flows down to rest
not on the "mountain," the powerful and learned,
but in the "valley," the unlearned and powerless
woman, herself.

Humanity's nature and destiny as bridal soul of
God is both symbolically feminine and also more
accessible to women, both in their modesty and

humility in society and also because it was to Eve that Christ gave the gifts of his capacity to love and honor God. Thus the gifts to Adam of power and wisdom are, in some way, more of a temptation to pride than a means of reuniting with God, than the gifts given to women. But Mechthild can also speak of the soul as God's image as masculine as well as feminine: as virile man in battle, as comely maiden at court before her lord, and as pleasing bride in the nuptial bed with God.[25] When Mechthild speaks of Adam or "man" collectively, it is with the male pronoun but with the assumption that women share equally in this human nature, in its nobility and its fall.

In speaking of her writing, Mechthild mentions the surprise of her scribe, Heinrich, at the "masculine style" of her book.[26] Despite her protests that she, "a sinful woman," is only following the commands of God in writing her revelations, this passage suggests that, to her foes and friends alike, Mechthild was not their notion of gentle, humble womanhood but appeared unnaturally masculine as she battled for her right to record her visions and to follow her own course of life, responding to her critics with fierce denunciations of their faults.

Masculinity and femininity are, thus, fluid categories for Mechthild. Women possess God's image equally with men. They have in no way a lesser nobility or capacity for spiritual interchange with God. Indeed, in some way, they are in a superior position, because they are less tempted by worldly power and have a natural affinity for the love relation with God for which the soul was created and in which it finds it consummation. This consummation, although tasted fleetingly while the soul remains tied to the fallen body, will be completed after death, when the body no longer ties down the soul.

After the Day of Judgment, the soul will receive back its original unfallen body. Following the "noble youth, Jesus Christ, the pure maiden's child," as comely and full of love as he was at eighteen, God's bridal souls, adorned with the wreaths of their virtues, will be carried to the eternal wedding with the Trinity. The "the highest dance of praise begins . . . from bliss to love, from love to joy, from joy to clarity, from clarity to power, from power to the highest heights." There they are greeted by the Father: "Rejoice dear Brides, My Son will embrace you. My divinity infuse you. My Holy Spirit will lead you always further in blissful vision, according to your will. What more could you wish for?"[27]

Julian of Norwich

With Julian of Norwich we move to the fourteenth century into the thriving city of Norwich, England. We also encounter a third form of religious life for women, the anchoress. Julian (her religious name, taken from the church of Saint Julian to which her anchorhold was attached)[1] was born about December of 1342, probably to a prosperous family of Norwich.[2] She must have adopted a serious devotional life as a young person, for she tells us that she had prayed for three gifts from God: to see Christ's passion as if she were actually present; a sickness to the point of death; and three wounds, contrition, compassion, and a full-hearted longing for God.[3] Such prayers express the desire to be totally focused on the relation to God in Christ, in the presence of Christ's passion and as if at the point of the consummation of her own life.[4]

Beginning on May 8, 1373, when Julian tells us she was "thirty and a half years old," she experienced the answer to these prayers. For seven days she lay ill to death.[5] Beginning on the seventh day (May 13) she experienced sixteen "shewings" of Christ's dying on the cross, as well as of God's relation to and love for us.[6] Having seen Christ's suffering in vivid detail to the final point of expiration, suddenly he was transformed into risen life; so she too was suddenly restored to health.[7] Perhaps shortly after this experience, Julian wrote down these visions, the interpretations given to her of them, and her first reflections on them, in a text of twenty-five chapters. She spent the next twenty years pondering the meaning of these visions and writing a much expanded version of her *Shewings of God's Love*.[8] The former is known as the "short text"; the latter is known as the "long text."

It is not known when she actually entered into the life of an anchoress, but it is likely that she did so shortly after these visions, the solitude of the anchorhold giving her the space for a dedicated life of prayer, study, and reflection on them.[9] The life Julian chose as an anchoress attached to the Church of Saint Julian at Norwich meant that she was enclosed in a room for the rest of her life, never to emerge until her death. But it was not an isolated or miserable life. A window into the church allowed her to participate in the liturgy, and another window into an attached parlor allowed her to counsel many who came seeking her advice and prayers, such as Margery of Kempe, who records her visit to Julian about 1412–13.[10]

Donations and local religious authorities provided for her physical needs, looked after by a servant and her assistant. It was expected that she would dress and be fed simply but adequately. So Julian's main task was to construct her own self-disciplined life of prayer and meditation.[11] Norwich was well-supplied with good religious libraries, including that of the Augustinian friars across from her church, and so it is likely that Julian's daily routine included the extended study of theological classics.[12] The church sat at a busy crossroads linking Conisford with the center of Norwich. Julian was there perhaps for more than forty years during a tumultuous time of war and plague.[13] Although set apart in her cell, Julian would receive the outpourings of daily troubles from those who came seeking her counsel. Such a holy woman was highly regarded by her contemporaries as one whose presence benefited the whole community.

Like Hildegard and Mechthild, Julian also felt the need to justify her extraordinary visions and her writing as a woman normally excluded from higher theological education and public teaching authority. She does so by describing herself as a "woman, ignorant, feeble and frail," yet nevertheless commanded to write what she has experienced because God has chosen her to be a conduit of God's teachings for the benefit of the whole Christian people, and in no way simply to exalt herself. As she puts it: "Because I am a woman should I therefore believe that I ought not to tell you about the goodness of God since I saw at the same time that it is His will that it be known?"[14] It is not she who teaches, but Jesus who teaches through her.

Her description of herself as "leued" (ignorant) and "vnlettyrde" have puzzled commentators,[15] since Julian's writing shows a woman of high literary skill in her Middle English dialect and considerable theological sophistication. It probably should be read to mean that she was self-taught beyond the elementary school level, thus not schooled in the Latin scholasticism of universities (not available to her).[16] It also expresses a typical self-disparagement by which medieval women claimed their authority by claiming it not in their own names but in the name of God, who had chosen to make them God's instrument.

Yet Julian does not simply supersede her own voice with the divine voice, but distinguishes between what has been revealed to her in visions and in words by formed divine inspiration in her understanding and her own pondering on questions for which she has an as yet incomplete understanding. Thus she often qualifies her reflections by phrases such as "as I see it" or "as I understand it."[17] Julian draws her theological reflection from three sources: natural reason, the common teaching of holy church (Scripture and tradition), and the inward workings of the Holy Spirit, which she sees as parts of one whole, "for these three are all from one God."[18] There is no indication that she felt incapable in any of these three areas as a woman. Indeed, aside from the brief justifications of her authority just cited, she does not discuss herself as a woman, but operates simply as a human person fully engaged in living the redemptive life, seeking to understand it and to share the benefits of her insights with the Christian people.

The central message that Julian understands to have been revealed by Christ's revelations to her is that of absolute assurance that God's persisting love for humans will triumph over all evil, that "all shall be well."[19] Julian's own central question to Christ is, "How can this be?" in the light of so much sin and suffering in the world and the church's teachings that many sinners will fail to repent and will be ultimately damned. The questions of theodicy—how an all-loving and all-powerful God could have allowed humans to fall in the first place, why evil continues and whether it will be fully overcome—fuel a lifetime of theological ponderings from which Julian emerges with a profound theological understanding of the basic categories of Christian faith, at once traditional and original.[20]

Not only is the Trinitarian God all-good in every way; the God whom Julian comes to name as Father, Mother, and Lord has created a world and formed human persons as the apex of creation in a way that fully manifests this divine goodness. For Julian all that is, is God; God is the true substance and being of all that is created. Nothing has being except through participation in the being of God. Because all that is manifests the being of God, all that is is good in its true nature. Evil has no substantial reality.[21]

Yet evil surely exists; and indeed, for Julian, it is the central theological problem. How can it be reconciled with this revelation of unmixed divine goodness in which all creation participates as its true "ground of being"? Here Julian differentiates the human being as *substance* and as *sensuality*, terms we might translate as essence and existence, rather than as soul and body.[22] As substance the human being is the image of God, the created manifestation of divine being, and so is completely good, by nature united to God's being. But, as sensuality, human existence has a certain autonomy that can be grasped in its created state as an end in itself, apart from God. When humans do this they fall into alienation from God and from themselves; human psychosomatic existence becomes split from its substance or true nature united to God. Although Julian does not dwell on the story of Adam's fall,[23] and never mentions Eve, one can infer that she assumes that this split of substance from sensuality results in a loss of an original immortality and perfection that humans would have enjoyed when their physical existence was united to their spiritual substance in union with God's uncreated being.[24]

This fall into sin (alienation) is manifest in woundedness. Humans experience every distress of mind and body. For Julian, sin, while "nothing" in itself, is felt in human life as *pain*[25]—the pains of mental anguish, self-blame, shame, and of physical suffering of the mortal body. Significantly, Julian never describes sin in terms of either pride or pleasure. For her there seems to be neither self-esteem nor delight in the sinful state. Rather, the primary way in which humans are caught in bondage to sin is in their self-absorption in their own distress, physical and mental. This distress leads them to forget their true nobility as God's image, and God's continuing love for them, and to slide into a despairing sense of hopelessness and worthlessness.

Julian insists that God is not angry with us and does not blame us for our fall into sin. These negative emotions are our own projections onto God from the context of our encapsulation in the fallen state where we see only our own dilemmas and fail to recognize that God continues to love us and to wish us only good. The supreme expression of God's "courteous" love is that God, the Son, from whom we have our substance, together with the whole Trinitarian God, also chooses to take on our sensuality, our bodily existence. Descending not only into the body, but taking on all the woundedness to death of the fallen human condition, Christ provides the conditions for our restoration to union with God and with our own true selves, indeed in a higher form than if we had remained in our original innocence.

God permitted and continues to permit humans to fall into sin because God allows humans freedom; moreover, in order for humans to attain their full spiritual maturity in union with God, they also have to experience what it means to fall out of that union into the distressful condition of separation from God.[26] But God has never ceased to love us and to sustain us in being, even as we became blind to this sustaining love. God, from the beginning, intended to provide the remedy. Divine Wisdom, from whom we have our spiritual substance, took on our bodily existence and bore all its woes in the crucifixion. Thereby God provides the means by which we can heal our division, "oning" our souls to God and drawing our sensuality back into union with our souls, anticipating the day when this union will be complete and every form of mortality and distress will cease.

Julian develops this theology of human fall and redemption through a parable of the fallen servant.[27] The servant, who is Adam and all humans, stands before his loving Lord eager to do God's will. This eagerness to obey is his true nature and impulse. But, in his alacrity to please God, he rushes off at top speed and falls into a ditch, where he becomes wounded, torn, and muddied. He then becomes so absorbed in his shame and distress that he fails to look up and see that his Lord has in no way stopped loving him. He moans in fear, imagining that God is angry with him, and so the servant is unable to recognize God's continuing love and gracious goodwill for him.

How does the servant break out of this dilemma and recognize both God's continuing love and his own continuing worth as God's true child and created image? This is possible only through God's greatest work of mercy. God as second person of the Trinity becomes the servant, "falling" into the "womb of the virgin," taking on the torn and muddied body of the fallen servant and bearing all its distresses. Christ now stands beside the loving Lord, carrying all rescued servants as his crown of glory. Through Christ's supreme act of love, the servant is restored to his position of honor before his Lord.

Christ, as creator of our soul and body, takes on the distresses of our fallen bodily condition— but without sin (separation from God). This, then, is Julian's answer to the problem of evil. But it is not simply that Christ has remedied our fall through entering our fallen bodily condition, but also that the sinful condition itself continually points us to the means of our healing. Because sin is experienced as pain, we cannot rest in sin but are continually impelled by our distress to seek to overcome it. The pains of sin purge and purify us and stir up repentance, compassion for others in pain, and a desire to find our true rest, which we can find only by resting in God.

Thus, for Julian, the wounds of sin are at the same time the medicines of sin, for our true nature remains that of God's created image.[28] We are never really separated from God, nor do we ever lose our true nature as God's created image. We have become blind and have forgotten who we are, but we have not ceased to be, in our true essence, the noble manifestation of God's loving goodness. Thus our quest to overcome the distresses caused by sin can only find its true solution as we awaken to a recognition of God's continuing love and are led back to God as the true ground of our nature and only real happiness.

The pains caused by sin, rightly understood in the light of God's continuing love, not only become means of purgation and healing, but also a means of participating with Christ in the healing of the sins of humanity. By bearing our pains in union with Christ, we become partners with Christ in redemption.[29] Thus Julian's vision of redemption is never of the isolated self seeking its own flight to God, but of a human being whose healing union with God is at the same time expressed in outpouring compassion for others, become a servant for others as Christ has become for us.[30]

Yet the dilemma of the ultimate resolution of evil remains for Julian. How can be it that *all* will be well, when evil and suffering continue to abound—as she herself could plainly see even from her anchorhold—in a society torn by plague, famine, war and division, even in the church? Julian does not contest the church's teaching that damnation awaits the unrepentant sinner, yet she holds out a belief that the mystery of God's love is still incomplete.[31] At the end, when our healed union with God and ourselves is completed and all sin and suffering are overcome, there will be a transformation that we do not yet fully know. We can be assured that God's love indeed means that *all* will be well, but here and now this truth must be held in faith rather than in full understanding.[32]

Julian's exploration of the Trinitarian nature of God as both mother and father has aroused renewed interest in modern times, especially among feminist theologians. Although both patristic and medieval theologians occasionally speak of God as mother, particularly in connection with Christ, through whom we are both reborn and fed through the Eucharist, Julian develops this maternal aspect of God the Son far more fully than any previous theologians.[33] In eleven chapters in the long text she elaborates on this union of fatherhood, motherhood, and lordship in God:[34]

> Thus in our making God almighty is our kindly Father and God all-wisdom is our kindly Mother, with the love and goodness of the Holy Spirit, which is all one God, one Lord. . . . Furthermore I saw that the second Person who is our Mother substantially, the same dear person is now become our Mother sensually. For of God's making we are double; that is to say, substantial and sensual. Our substance

is that higher part which we have of our Father, God almighty. And the second Person of the Trinity is our Mother in kind, in our substantial making—in whom we are grounded and rooted; and he is our Mother of mercy in taking our sensuality. And thus our Mother means for us different manners of his working, in whom our parts are kept unseparated. For in our Mother Christ we have profit and increase; and in mercy he reforms and restores us; and by the power of our passion, his death and his uprising, oned us to our substance. Thus our Mother in mercy works to all his beloved children who are docile and obedient to him. . . . Thus Jesus Christ who does good against evil is our very Mother. We have our being of him, where every ground of Motherhood begins, with all the sweet keeping of love that endlessly follows. As truly as God is our Father, so truly is God our Mother.[35]

Julian's exploration of God's motherhood is rooted in key aspects of her theology. The persons of the Trinity are for her a dynamic relationship not just with each other, but with us. We are created, restored, and brought to fulfillment in interrelationship with God as Father, Mother, and Lord. Her identification of the Second Person with Wisdom reclaims the feminine aspect of this biblical symbol.[36] She also uses the traditional christological symbols of baptism and Eucharist to see Christ as the one in whom we are reborn and fed, as a mother brings a child forth from her womb and feeds it from her own body.[37] But central to her view of God as Mother as well as Father is her understanding of divine love as incapable of real anger or rejection of God's children, no more than a mother could reject her child, even though she might need to appear stern at times to discipline it. But behind even this discipline is a love that can never cease. Julian sees this kind of divine love as motherlike, or rather divine Motherhood as its fullest reality, which we see palely revealed in human mothers.[38]

While this sense of God's motherhood reflects something of Julian's experience of women as mothers (or at least her view of what a mother's love should be), her understanding of sin also reflects a significant shift in perspective that perhaps also reflects her experience as a woman. In sharp contrast to the Augustinian view of sin as overweening pride and concupiscence, Julian views our bondage to sin primarily as our entrapment in an overwhelming sense of fear and worthlessness and as manifest in pain, not pleasure. But once we glimpse God's continuing love and our own worth in God's eyes, we can become secure in our trust in God. Our wounds can become our medicines for growth in contrition, compassion for our fellow Christians, and reunion with God and with our own true selves. Or as she puts it at the end of the short text: "For God wants us always to be strong in our love and peaceful and restful as he is towards us, and he wants us to be, for ourselves and for our fellow Christians, what he is for us."[39]

Notes

INTRODUCTION

1 For example, Jerome, Epistle 48, *Letters of St. Jerome*, trans. C. C. Mierow (Westminster, Md.: Newman Press, 1963).

2 See Andrew Kadel, *Matrology: A Bibliography of Writings by Christian Women from the First to the Fifteenth Centuries* (New York: Continuum, 1995), 38–57.

3 One letter preserved as a letter of Jerome urging Marcella to visit the holy land was probably from Paula and Eustochium; ibid., 55.

4 Jerome, Epistle 127.7; see Rosemary R. Ruether, "Misogynism and Virginal Feminism in the Fathers of the Church," in *Religion and Sexism: Images of Women in the Jewish and Christian Traditions*, R. R. Ruether, ed. (New York: Simon and Schuster, 1974), 175.

5 For example, the four prophet daughters of Philip (Acts 21:9). Despite the suppression of the Montanist women prophets in the second century, the Jewish tradition of women prophets, as well as the Pentecostal narrative in which women are included in the prophetic gift (Acts 2:17–18), laid the basis in Christianity for the tradition that women could be prophets.

6 For the literature on the trial of Joan of Arc, see Kadel, *Matrology*, 142–45.

HILDEGARD OF BINGEN

1 See "Declaration," in *Scivias*, Columba Hart and Jane Bishop, translators (New York: Paulist Press, 1990), 59–60; see also the Epilogue of her *Book of Divine Works*, where Hildegard declares that her words came from divine revelation to a "simple and uneducated woman":

> Therefore, let no one be so rash as to alter in any way the content of this book—either by adding to it or by diminishing it by omissions—lest such a person be blotted out of the book of life and out of all good fortune under the sun! There is but one exception to this rule—the editing of words or sentences that have been put down too simply under the inspiration of the Holy Spirit. But anyone who presumed to make changes for other reasons will sin against the Holy Spirit and will not be forgiven in this world or the next.

Hildegard of Bingen's Book of Divine Works with Letters and Songs, Matthew Fox, ed. (Santa Fe, N.M.: Bear and Co., 1987), 266. For the Latin text of the sections of these two works, see *Patrologia Latina*, J. P. Migne, ed. (Paris: 1855), vol. 197, column 383–86 and 1037–38. A revised Latin edition of the *Scivias* is available, edited by Adelgundis Fuhrkotter in the *Corpus Christianorum* (Turnhout: Brepols, 1978), vols. 43 and 43A. Hildegard probably had wide reading in the church fathers, but not formal training; see Barbara Newman's introduction to the Hart and Bishop translation of the *Scivias*, 44. For her secret language or *lingua ignota*, see Barbara New-man, *Saint Hildegard of Bingen's Symphonia* (Ithaca, N.Y.: Cornell University Press, 1988), 18.

2 The Latin text of the *Vita* is found in *Patrologia Latina*, vol. 197, columns 93–130, as well as a more recent edition by Monica Klae in *Corpus Christianorum* (Turnhout: Brepols, 1993), vol. 126. There is a German translation by A. Fuhrkotter, *Das Leben der HI. Hildegard von Bingen* (Dusseldorf, 1968). The only complete English transla-tion is by H. Silvas in the journal *Tjurunga: Australian Benedictine Review* 29 (1985): 4–25; 30 (1986): 63–73; 31 (1986): 31–41; and 32 (1987): 46–59.

3 *Ut mortem inferre minentur*: in letter 103R, 1.76, to Guil-bert of Gembloux describing her experiences of revela-tion and illness. The modern Latin edition of the letters of Hildegard is appearing in *Corpus Christianorum*, L. Van Acker, ed. (Turnhout: Brepols, 1991, 1993). Letter 103R appears in vol. 91A, 258–65. An English translation of the Van Acker edition was translated by Joseph L. Baird and Radd K. Erhman (New York: Oxford Univer-sity Press, 1994), but this volume only covers the first volume of the Van Acker edition to letter 90. English translations of letters 103R are in Matthew Fox's edi-tion of the *Book of Divine Works with Letters and Songs*, 347–51 (there it is spelled Wibert of Gembloux), and in *Hildegard of Bingen: Mystical Writings*, Fiona Bowie and Oliver Davies, eds. (New York: Crossroad, 1990), 143–46.

4 *Vita*; see excerpt in Bowie and Davies, 64. Hildegard's illnesses probably had a physiological basis, but they also seem closely related to her visions and to the thwarting of her self-expression (Newman, *Saint Hildegard*, 7–11, 129). She continually reports that she became paralyzed by pain when she was blocked from expressing and act-ing on her visions, but this pain was relieved when she

won her way. Unlike later medieval women mystics, Hildegard's health was probably not impaired by severe asceticism. She practiced the Benedictine tradition of moderation, and her works of medicine, *Liber Simplicis Medicinae* and *Causae et Curae*, show a strong respect for the principle of balance in good health. In a letter to the younger woman mystic Elisabeth of Schönau, she warns her against impairing her health by excessive fasting; see *Divine Works*, Fox, ed., 340–42.

5 "Declaration," *Scivias*, see Hart and Bishop translation, 59.

6 The earliest manuscript of the *Scivias* to survive to modern times was prepared about 1165 in the Rupertsberg scriptorium, illuminated with thirty-five miniatures with vivid colors and gold and silver leaf. They were done by artists under Hildegard's personal direction. Unfortunately this original manuscript disappeared during the bombing of Dresden in 1945, but a photocopy was made in 1927 and a hand-painted facsimile was made by the nuns of Eibingen in 1927–33. See Barbara Newman's introduction to the *Scivias*, 25–26. The Fuhrkotter edition of the *Scivias* in *Corpus Christianorum*, vols. 43–43A has excellent full-color reproductions of these miniatures.

7 For the parallel of Hildegard's *Scivias* with the topics of other twelfth-century summae, such as Hugh of St. Victor's *On the Sacraments of the Christian Church*, see Newman's introduction to the *Scivias*, 23–24.

8 See, for example, letter 77R, probably originally a sermon delivered at Saint Disibod, which Hildegard sent to Abbott Helengerus there about 1170; in this letter she summarizes the whole salvation history in a few pages. Latin: Van Acker, 168–75; English: Baird and Ehrman, 166–72.

9 The term appears as formulaic in Hildegard's letters to her correspondents as well as her other writings. For

discussion, see Barbara Newman, *Sister of Wisdom: St. Hildegard's Theology of the Feminine* (Berkeley: University of California Press, 1987), 1–41.

10 Dean Philip of Cologne (letter 15), in reporting Hildegard's sermon at Cologne, says: "We were greatly astonished that God works through such a fragile vessel, such a fragile sex, to display the great marvels of His secrets, but the 'Spirit breatheth where he will' (John 3:8)." This text is also cited by Arnold, archbishop of Mainz, with 1 Cor. 12:11 (the Spirit allots gifts to each as the Spirit chooses); Amos 7:14 (God made a tiller of fields into a prophet); and Num. 22:28 (God made an ass speak); to explain how God might choose a woman as a prophet (letter 20): in Van Acker, 33, 56; Baird and Ehrman, 54, 71–72.

11 Hildegard uses various terms to refer to the humble matter of the human body, sometimes describing it negatively in a way that suggests its sinful expression ("ashes of ashes and filth of filth": *cinis cineris et putredo putredinis: Scivias, Patrologia Latina*, vol. 197, column 383A; "filthy black mire": *limum nigrum et lutulentum*, column 565A, and sometimes more neutrally as "a little lump of wet clay": *parvam glebam limosae terrae*: columns 441C, 445A).

12 Letter 201R (in Van Acker, vol. 91A, 456–57). See English translation in Bowie and Davies, 130–31.

13 Ibid.

14 In her letter to Guilbert of Gembloux, who asked about the nature of her revelatory experience, Hildegard says that she experiences a light through which she sees the reflection of God, which is known to her as the "reflection of the Living Light," but occasionally she experiences the Living Light directly. When this happens her feelings of sorrow and perplexity drain away and she feels like a young girl and not an old woman (*more*

simplicis puelle, et non uetule mulieris habeam): letter 103R, Van Acker, 262, lines 101–2.

15 *Istus tempus muliebre est, quia iustitia Dei debilis est. Sed fortitudo iustitie Dei exsudet, et bellatrix contra iniustitiam exsistit, quatenus deuicta cadat*: letter 23, Van Acker, 65–6, lines 158–61. English translation: Baird and Ehrman, 79.

16 Letter 1 and reply: Van Acker, vol. 91, 3–7, and Baird and Ehrman, 28–31.

17 *Vita* 1, 4, in Klaes, *Corpus Christianorum*, vol. 126, 9–10. See also letter 2 to Pope Eugenius (Van Acker, 7–8; Baird and Ehrman, 32–33).

18 The letters of Frederick Barbarossa have not yet appeared in the Van Acker Latin edition. Van Acker follows the traditional ordering of Hildegard's letters in which they appear by rank and then alphabetically by place, starting with ecclesiastical rank and then moving to laypeople by rank, so letters to kings will appear only in section 4, letters 311–31. These letters were published in J. B. Pitra, *Analecta Sanctae Hildegardis, Analecta Sacra*, vol. 8 (Monte Cassino, 1882). Matthew Fox has two of Hildegard's letters to Frederick (289–92). The German translation by Adelgundis Fuhrkotter, *Hildegard van Bingen, Briefwechsel* (Salzburg: Otto Müller Verlag, 1990) has one letter of Frederick Barbarossa to Hildegard and four letters of Hildegard to Frederick, 81–87.

19 *Vita* (Bowie and Davies, 66).

20 *Tu ergo, o homo, . . . scribe quae uides at audis*: Fuhrkotter, *Corpus Christianorum*, 5, lines 75–78 (*Patrologia Latina*, 386). For discussion see Edward Peter Nolan, *Cry Out and Write: A Feminine Poetics of Revelation* (New York: Continuum, 1994), 55–135.

21 For paradise and the fall, see *Scivias*, Book 2, vision 1 (Hart and Bishop, 149–57). For an example of Hildegard's

use of the terms "moistness" and "greenness," see section 8 of this vision, where she says that God gave Adam the power of the Holy Spirit to cling to the Word in moist, green fruitfulness: *adhaerentis eidem Verbo in umida uiriditate fructuositatis* (Fuhrkotter, *Corpus Christianorum*, vol. 43, 116, lines 237–38).

22 Letter 23 to the prelates of Mainz (Baird and Ehrman, 76–79; Van Acker, 61–66). See also Newman, *Symphonia*, 18–25.

23 See Newman, *Sister of Wisdom*, 111–12.

24 For Lucifer's fall, see *Scivias* 2, vision 2, and 3, vision 1 (Hart and Bishop), 73–76 and 317–21. Also lee letter 31R (Baird and Ehrman, 95–99).

25 *Scivias*, 3, vision 1 (Hart and Bishop, 147–48, 153); also see discussion in Newman, *Sister of Wisdom*, 168–69.

26 *Scivias* 2, vision 3 (Hart and Bishop, 177–78).

27 See Pamela Sheingorn, "The Virtues in Hildegard's *Ordo Virtutem*, or, It Was a Woman's World," in *The Ordo Virtutem of Hildegard of Bingen*, Audrey E. Davidson, ed. (Kalamazoo, Mich.: Western Michigan University Press, 1992), 43–62.

28 For example, *Scivias* 2, vision 1, where God addresses her in these words: "O diffident mind, who are taught inwardly by mystical inspiration, though because of Eve's transgression you are trodden on by the masculine sex (*quamuis conculcata sis per uirilem formam propter praeuaricationem Euae*), speak of that fiery work this sure vision has shown you" (Hart and Bishop, 150; Fuhrkotter, *Corpus Christianorum*, vol. 43, 112, lines 104–5).

29 *Scivias* 1, vision 2, sections 11–12 (Hart and Bishop, 77–79).

30 *Scivias* 2, vision 6, sections 76–77 (Hart and Bishop, 276).

31 Letter 52 and reply (Baird and Ehrman, 127–30; Van Acker, 125–30); also *Scivias* 3, vision 6, sections 16–17 (Hart and Bishop, 396).

32 *Book of Divine Works* 1, vision 4, which delineates the microcosm-macrocosm relation between the human body-soul and the dynamic relations of the cosmos. In section 100 we read:

> God gave the first man a helper in the form of woman, who is man's mirror image and in her the whole human race was present in a latent way. . . . Man and woman are in this way so involved with each other that one of them is the work of the other. Neither of them could therefore live without the other. Man signifies the divinity, while woman signifies humanity of the Son of God (*Et vir divinitatem, femina vero humanitatem Filii Dei significant*).

> *Patrologia Latina*, vol. 197, column 885C.

33 *Book of Divine Works* 1, vision 1 on Wisdom in Creation; 3, vision 8 on Love and vision 9 on Creation and Wisdom's garment. For discussion, see Newman, *Wisdom's Sister*, 42–88.

34 *Book of Divine Works* 1, vision 1, 17, which parallels the virgin earth and the Virgin Mary.

35 *Scivias* 2, vision 6 (Hart and Bishop, 231–38).

36 *Scivias* 2, visions 4 and 5 (Hart and Bishop, 187–234).

37 *Scivias* 3, vision 11 (Hart and Bishop, 491–511).

38 Letter 52R (Baird and Ehrman, 128–30).

39 Letter 23 (Baird and Ehrman, 79).

40 Ibid.

41 See *Scivias* 2, vision 6, sections 62–70. Hildegard interprets 1 Tim. 3:2, 12 on bishops and deacons having one wife to mean that the church is the wife of the clergy

and so to take a human wife would be bigamy: Hart and
Bishop, 274. In 2, vision 5, the figure of chastity is pictured at the center of the church's bosom as the key to
her ministries (Hart and Bishop, 199–216).

42 *Scivias* 2, vision 5, section 23 on the role of married laypeople in the church who lie in the "clouds" around the
church's navel (Hart and Bishop, 214–15).

43 *Scivias* 3, vision 12, section 8 (Hart and Bishop, 518).

44 See Ida Raming, *The Exclusion of Women from Priesthood: Divine Law or Sex Discrimination?* (Metuchen,
N.J.: Scarecrow Press, 1976), 7.

45 See letter 10 to Pope Athanasius and Hildegard's reply
(Baird and Ehrmann, 45–47; Van Acker, 23–25).

46 See letter 15R (Baird and Ehrmann, 54–63; Van Acker,
34–47).

47 *The Letters of Catherine of Siena*, Suzanne Noffke, ed.
(Binghamton, N.Y.: Medieval and Renaissance Texts and
Studies, 1988).

48 Mary J. Finnegan, *Women of Helfta: Scholars and Mystics*
(Athens: University of Georgia Press, 1991).

MECHTHILD OF MAGDEBURG

1 Mechthild von Magdeburg, *The Flowing Light of the God-
head*, book 5.24. English edition: translated by Christiane
Mesch Galvani, ed. with introduction by Susan Clark
(New York: Garland, 1991), 152–54. German edition:
Mechthild von Magdeburg, *Das Fliessende Licht der Gott-
heit*, Hans Neumann, ed. (Munich and Zurich: Artemis
Verlag, 1990), 181–83.

2 Mechthild, book 4.2; Galvani, 96; Neumann, 110.

3 For the general history of the Beguines, see Ernest W.
McDonnell, *The Beguines and Beghards in Medieval*

Culture (New Brunswick, N.J.: Rutgers University Press, 1954). See also B. Bolton, "Mulieres Sanctae," in *Sanctity and Secularity: The Church and the World*, D. Baker, ed. (Oxford: Blackwell, 1973), 77–95. For Mechthild's life as a Beguine, see Frank Tobin, *Mechthild van Magdeburg: A Medieval Mystic in Modern Eyes* (Columbia, S.C.: Camden House, 1991, 1995), 127–30.

4 The developing belief in purgatory gave women mystics and charismatics a new area of ministry in (1) visions that revealed the fate of souls after death, and (2) influence with God to pray souls out of purgatory into heaven. Hildegard of Bingen was asked about the fate of particular souls on several occasions. Mechthild of Magdeburg not only had visions of the fate of particular souls, but on several occasions intervened with God to pray large groups of souls out of purgatory. See book 2.7, where she influenced God's release of one thousand souls, and book 3.15, where she helped release seventy thousand souls. Mechthild did not seem to make a fixed distinction between hell and purgatory, but assumed traditions of suffering that ran from purgatory to hell and saw God as reaching down even into hell to have mercy on souls. For her such suffering after death reflects the soul's own chosen spiritual state, especially its failure to "sigh" (i.e., to repent); while God for her is utterly compassionate rather than punitive: See book 7.41. For a discussion, see Barbara Newman, "On the Threshold of Dead: Purgatory, Hell and Religious Women," in her *From Virile Woman to WomanChrist: Studies in Medieval Religion and Literature* (Philadelphia: University of Pennsylvania Press, 1995), 108–36.

5 Books 2.24, 4.2, 5.11, and 7.28: Galvani, 50, 96, 138, and 195.

6 See Prologue and book 1.1 of *The Flowing Light of the Godhead*.

7 The Low German original of Mechthild's book has not
been found. Around 1290 Heinrich of Halle, who col-
lected and organized the original Low German version,
translated it into Latin as *Lux Divinitatis fluens in corda
veritatis*. This version, on parchment, is in the university
library of Basel. About 1344–45 Henrich of Nordlingen
and the Friends of God in Basle made a translation of
the Low German text into Middle High German, the
only copy of which is in the library of the Benedictine
Monastery of Einsiedeln. This text, plus a free translation
into modern German, was published by Morel Gall in
1869. The best modern version of the fourteenth-century
text is edited by Hans Neumann, published in 1990 (see
note 55 above).

8 Book 2.26:

> *Das buch ist drivaltig und bezeichent alleine
> mich. Dis bermit, das hie umbe gat, bezeichent
> min reine, wisse, gerehte menscheit, die dur dich
> den tot leit. Do wort bezeichent mine wunderliche
> gotheit; du vliessent von* stunde ze stunde *in dine
> sele us von minem gotlichen munde. Du stimme der
> worten* bezeichtenet *minen lebendigen geist and
> vollebringet mit im selben die rehten warheit.*

Neumann, 68.

9 Book 2.26: Galvani, 56–57; Neumann, 68–69.

10 Galvani, 50; Neumann, 59.

11 For Mechthild's picture of the coming of the Antichrist
and the sufferings that will befall the saints at that time,
see particularly book 6.15 (Galvani, 182–86).

12 Barbara Newman, *From Virile Woman to WomanChrist*,
137–67.

13 Book 3.9: Galvani, 74.

14 Ibid.

15 Book 5.9: Galvani, 137. Mechthild is speaking here of the resurrection from the dead when the souls receive back their original unfallen bodies, without those qualities of "sinful human sap," which came to humans in general, and "cursed blood," which came to women, from eating the apple: *"Aber das sundige menschliche saf, das Adam us oppfel beis, das noch naturlich allu unsru lider durgat, und dar zu das verfluchte blut, das Even und allen wiben von dem oppfel entstunt, das wart inen nit wider gegeben"*: Neumann, 163. For the symbolism of liquids in Mechthild—water, blood, milk, and wine—and their relation to this particular passage, see James C. Franklin, *Mystical Transformations: The Imagery of Liquids in the Word of Mechthild of Magdeburg* (London: Associated University Presses, 1978).

16 Galvani, 15–16.

17 Book 1.3: Galvani, 8–9.

18 Book 1.4: Galvani, 9.

19 For example, book 2.2: "When the maiden pursues the youth eagerly, His noble nature is so willing that He receives her and she gladly leads Him as her heart desires" (Galvani, 29); book 2.22: "The worthiest angel, Jesus Christ, who soars above the Seraphim, who must be God undivided with His Father, that is whom I must take into my arms, to eat and drink Him and do with as I please" (Galvani, 47); book 2.25: Christ speaking to the soul, "And you shall have power over Me Myself. I am lovingly inclined to you" (Galvani, 54); book 4.15: Speaking of the highest state of love of God, "This state can only be attained when a complete exchange occurs with God, namely that you give God all that is yours, inwardly and outwardly, then will He truly give you what is His, inwardly and outwardly" (Galvani, 113); book 7.16: On the longing of the soul to be with God, God

replies to the soul, "Our Lord spoke: I have longed for you since the world began. I long for you, and you long for Me. When two fervent desires come together, love is perfected" (Galvani, 221).

20 Book 1.4: Galvani, 9.

21 Book 4.12: Galvani, 108–11.

22 Book 3.10: Galvani, 76–78.

23 Book 4.2: Galvani, 99. There are different views of the severity of the ascetic practices of bodily self-punishment. In this passage Mechthild clearly speaks of flagellation, as well as fasting and vigils, and says, "These were the weapons of my soul with which I conquered my body so successfully that for twenty years there was never a time when I was not tired, sick and weak." There is a suggestion that in her later years she was easier on her body and the sickness of older years was enough bodily suffering without special efforts to increase it. See Carolyn Bynum, *Jesus as Mother: Studies in the Spirituality of the High Middle Ages* (Berkeley: University of California Press, 1982), 231.

24 Book 1.29: Galvani, 18.

25 Book 2.19: Galvani, 41.

26 Book 5.12: "Meister Henrich, uch wundert *sumenlicher* worten, die in diesem buche gescriben sint": Neumann, 166.

27 Book 7.37: Galvani, 242–43.

JULIAN OF NORWICH

1 It was customary for an anchoress to adopt the name of the church to which she was attached. For the church of Saint Julian at Conisford, see Michael McLean, *Guide Book to St. Julian's Church and Lady Julian's Cell*

(Norwich, 1979). There is no record of Julian's original family and given names.

2 Julian's literacy, as well as the financial support necessary to support an anchoress, suggests both a prosperous family and good social connections. See Joan M. Nuth, *Wisdom's Daughter: The Theology of Julian of Norwich* (New York: Crossroads, 1991), 10.

3 Chapter 1, short text. For the Middle English text of the short and long texts, see *The Book of Showings to the Anchoress Julian of Norwich*, parts 1 and 2, Edmund Colledge, O.S.A., and James Walsh, S.J., eds. (Toronto: Pontifical Institute of Mediaeval Studies, 1978) (hereafter Colledge and Walsh). There are many modem English translations; I refer here primarily to *Julian of Norwich: Showings*, Edmund Colledge, O.S.A., and James Walsh, S.J. (New York: Paulist Press, 1979) (hereafter Colledge and Walsh, Paulist edition).

4 For an insightful interpretation of the three prayers, see Grace M. Jantzen, *Julian of Norwich: Mystic and Theologian* (London: SPCK, 1987).

5 Chapter 2, short text: Colledge and Walsh, part l, 207–9.

6 The sixteen showings described in the short text are summarized in the first chapter of the long text: Colledge and Walsh, Paulist edition, 175–77.

7 Chapters 2 and 10–12, short text: Colledge and Walsh, Paulist edition, 128–29 and 141–44.

8 In chapter 86 of the long text, Julian speaks of meditating on the visions for "fifteen years after and more"; in chapter 51 of the long text she speaks of receiving specific instruction on how to interpret the parable of the servant: "Twenty years after the time of the revelation except three months" (i.e., c. February 1393). This statement indicates that the parable of the servant was part of the original revelation, but Julian did not include it in the short text

because she was puzzled by its apparent contradiction of church teaching. This suggests a process of writing the long text beginning around 1388, but completing it only after February 1393, when she received the instruction on the meaning of the servant parable. See Colledge and Walsh, part 1, 18–25.

9 There is no evidence of when Julian entered the anchorhold. It was at least by 1393, when the first will given to support her in the anchorhold is dated. But most scholars think she probably entered it earlier, perhaps shortly after the visions of 1373, in order to meditate on them. See Colledge and Walsh, part 1, 33–35; also Jantzen, *Julian of Norwich*, 21–25.

10 *The Book of Margery of Kempe*, B. A. Windeatt (Harmondsworth, England: Penguin, 1985), 42.

11 The rule for the life of an anchorite is laid out in Ancrene Riwle, see E. J. Dobson, *The Origin of the Ancrene Wisse* (Oxford: Clarendon, 1976). For other rules see also Aelred Rievaulx, *Regula ad Sororem*, in *Treatises and Pastoral Prayers* (Kalamazoo, Mich.: Cistercian Publications, 1971). Also see discussion in Jantzen, *Julian of Norwich*, 28–48.

12 Colledge and Walsh suggest that Julian may have been a nun at the Benedictine community at Carrow before becoming an anchorite and so got a solid education there. They believe she knew Latin and had a good grounding in Latin Scripture, the Latin church fathers and liberal arts, as well as vernacular classics: see part 1, 43–59. Others, such as Jantzen, see her as more self-educated on the basis of her own reading; *Julian of Norwich*, 15–20.

13 The time when Julian lived in Norwich saw the ravages of the Black Plague, several major famines, the beginnings of the Hundred Years War, peasant revolts that sacked churches and monasteries, and the persecution and martyrdom of the Lollards: see Jantzen, *Julian of*

Norwich, 3–12. For the location of Saint Julian's Church in Conisford, see Norman P. Tanner, *The Church in Late Medieval Norwich*, 1370–1532 (Toronto: Pontifical Institute of Mediaeval Studies, 1984), xii.

14 Chapter 6, short text.

15 Colledge and Walsh, part 1, 222.41–42 and part 2, 285.2.

16 On Julian's education, see note 93 above. Also see Nuth, *Wisdom's Daughter*, 8–10.

17 For example, chapter 43, long text: "as to my syghte": Colledge and Walsh, part 2, 477.22; also chapter 65, long text: 627.2; chapter 73, long text: 666.2–8.

18 Chapter 80, long text; see discussion in Jantzen, *Julian of Norwich*, 95–106.

19 Versions of this phrase appear throughout the short and long texts; for example, chapter 15, short text: "I wille make alle thynge wele, I schalle make alle thynge wele, I maye make alle thynge wele and I can make alle thynge wele and powe schalle se pat thy selfe, that alle thynge schalle be wele": Colledge and Walsh, part 1, 249.2–5; also chapter 16, short text: part 1, 252.11–12 and chapter 27, long text: part 2, 405.13–14.

20 For the theodicy of Julian, see Denise N. Baker, *Julian of Norwich's Showings: From Vision to Book* (Princeton, N.J.: Princeton University Press, 1994), 63–82.

21 See chapter 23, short text, and chapters 11 and 27, long text.

22 Julian is not a precise philosophical thinker and so her discussion of the dualism between soul and body, interior and exterior, the godly and the beastly wills, and substance and sensuality do not always seem consistent. See chapters 19, 45, 55, and 64, long text. Jantzen sees Julian's distinction of substance and sensuality as best translated to mean essence and existence, rather than soul and body: see her *Julian of Norwich*, 127–61.

23 In chapter 14, short text, and chapter 29, long text, Adam's fall is discussed in terms of our assurance that God can forgive even the greatest sin, since God has already remedied the greatest sin possible, namely, Adam's fall.

24 In chapter 47, long text, Julian sees our inability to remain focused in blissful union with God in this present life, without falling back into feelings of separation, as the foundational expression of our fallen state, "the opposition that is in ourselves and that comes from the old root of our first sin"; Colledge and Walsh, Paulist edition, 261.

25 "But I did not see sin, for I believe that it has no kind of substance, no share in being, nor can it be recognized except by the pain caused by it"; chapter 27, long text: Colledge and Walsh, Paulist edition, 225; also Colledge and Walsh, part 2, 406.26–28.

26 Thus chapter 27, long text: "Sin is necessary, but all will be well"; also chapters 35 and 61, long text; see discussion in Margaret Ann Palliser, O.P., *Christ, Our Mother of Mercy: Divine Mercy and Compassion in the Theology of the Showings of Julian of Norwich* (New York: Walter de Gruyter, 1992), 102–6.

27 Chapter 51, long text; Julian says that it was twenty years, less three months, after the parable of the servant was revealed to her that she received the explanation of it. The interpretation of this parable is central to Julian's exploration of the problem of evil in relation to divine goodness; see Jantzen, *Julian of Norwich*, 190–96; also Nuth, *Wisdom's Daughter*, 44–54, and Baker, *Julian of Norwich's Showings*, 83–106.

28 See chapter 39, long text, where she speaks of the sinful soul being healed by the medicines of contrition, compassion, and longing for God, so that the wounds of sin are not seen by God as wounds but as honors; also chapter 56, long text, where she says that the pains caused by sin

will themselves be redemptive: "When our sensuality by the power of Christ's passion can be brought up into the substance, with all the profits of our tribulation which our Lord can make us obtain through mercy and grace"; Colledge and Walsh, Paulist edition, 289.

29 Thus chapter 43, long text: "For he (God) beholds us in love and wants to make us partners in his good will and work"; Colledge and Walsh, Paulist edition, 253.

30 Julian has a strong sense of solidarity with the human community, for whom we should seek to do good but not spend our time in judgmental scrutiny of other's sins; e.g., chapter 79, long text: "I was taught that I ought to see my own sin and not other men's, unless it may be for the comfort and help of my fellow Christians" (Colledge and Walsh, Paulist edition, 334).

31 Chapter 32, long text; also chapter 46, long text.

32 Chapter 27, long text.

33 See Baker, *Julian of Norwich's Showings*, 107–34; also Bynum, *Jesus as Mother*; Ritamary Bradley, "Patristic Background of the Motherhood Similitude in Julian of Norwich," *Christian Scholar's Review* 8 (1978): 101–13; Jennifer Heimmel, "God Is Our Mother: Julian of Norwich and the Medieval Image of Christian Feminine Divinity," *Elizabethan and Renaissance Studies* 92:5 (Salzburg: Institute für Anglistik und Amerikanistick, Universität Salzburg, 1982).

34 Chapters 52–62, long text.

35 Chapters 58, 59, long text: translation from James Walsh (New York: Harper and Row, 1961), 159–61.

36 See Baker, *Julian of Norwich's Showings*, 122–23.

37 Chapter 60, long text.

38 Ibid.

39 Chapter 25, short text: Colledge and Walsh, Paulist edition, 170.

Further Reading

Hildegard of Bingen, *Scivias*, trans. Columba Hart and Jane Bishop. New York: Paulist Press, 1990.

Hildegard of Bingen: Mystical Writings, ed. Fiona Bowie and Oliver Davies. New York: Crossroad, 1990.

Hildegard of Bingen's Book of Divine Works with Letters and Songs, ed. Matthew Fox. Santa Fe, N.M.: Bear & Co., 1987.

Grace M. Jantzen. *Julian of Norwich: Mystic and Theologian*. London: SPCK, 1987.

Julian of Norwich: Showings, ed. Edmund Colledge, O.S.A., and James Walsh, S.J. New York: Paulist, 1979.

Shawn Madigan, C.S.J. *Mystics, Visionaries, and Prophets: A Historical Anthology of Women's Spiritual Writings*. Minneapolis: Fortress Press, 1998.

Mechtild of Magdeburg. *The Flowing Light of the Godhead*, trans. Christiane Mesch Galvani, ed. Susan Clark. New York: Garland, 1991.

Rosemary Radford Ruether. *Women and Redemption: A Theological History*. Minneapolis: Fortress Press, 1998.